BEGIN

Books available by Brendan Kennelly

Brendan Kennelly

BEGIN

BLOODAXE BOOKS

ISBN: 1 85224 497 6

First published 1999 by
Bloodaxe Books Ltd,
P.O. Box 1SN,
Newcastle upon Tyne NE99 1SN.

Bloodaxe Books Ltd acknowledges
the financial assistance of Northern Arts.

Cover printing by J. Thomson Colour Printers Ltd, Glasgow.

Printed in Great Britain by
Cromwell Press Ltd, Trowbridge, Wiltshire.

for Derry and Jeanne Jeffares

Contents

The Field of Cries

Late Imitators

ECHOING NOTE

Poetry is a land and sea of echoes connecting with each other and with listening hearts as the years work and dream themselves into extinction. These echoes are the consequences of calm, irrefutable and ultimately unanswerable obsessions that quietly haunt sleeping and waking hours. Poetry can be a kind of beautiful tyranny that eats your life away. It's more predatory than it's usually given credit for. It forces you to look at your obsessive dreams and voices, to listen to them, to write them down as they bid you. They will not be resisted.

This tyranny is the source of poetry's shocking democracy; everyone who has ever loved, hated, killed, worked, been idle, been wounded, has exploited or been exploited deserves a voice, *should* have a voice. Why is this pressing, relentless tyranny the source of a shocking democracy, an imaginative lust for justice? I don't know. But I know the connection is there since the day a man in a Dublin street said to me I should be hanged for writing *The Book of Judas*. I knew he didn't want to let the Judas in himself find expression. Any style is a risk and a commitment; it is potentially undermining and insulting; it involves the possibility of going astray, or of being led astray by language, or by one's own use of language. Language uses poets more frequently and perhaps more revealingly than poets use language. And the laughter of language as it wreaks revenge on certain of its users is like the way a bomb laughs as it explodes in a busy street. Why and how does a bomb talk? I've tried to face this in 'Hear the voice of the bomb'.

The echopower of poetry is steppingstones across a river of time, it makes connections and sets up reverberations where there was only the consolation of ordinary emptiness. The poems in this book, many of them, seem to me to be echopoems. They were written and re-written over a period of almost forty years. Anyone who has read my attempts to give voices to people and phenomena that should not have voices in our culture will know what I mean when I say that echoes combat emptiness. Echoes of violence, childhood, love, history, words, madness, sickness, learning, weather, betrayal, politicians, friends, silence, songs, killers with causes, famine, the dead, gossip, cries, begrudgery, streets, mistakes, rooms, self-communicating mutterers, traffic, mythology, faces, loneliness, hatred, prayer, money, translation, greed, risking existence, storytellers, eyes, drinkers, hurts, laughter, families, sounds, memories, conversation, poets, rivers, saints, devils, curses, blessings, and the recurring hints of some hope in self-renewal, of recognising that the real tragedy is simply giving up, of refusing the shakey hope of beginning again – these are echoes creating further echoes.

If a bomb has a voice, does it not follow that a kindly, articulate altruism is the highest form of intelligence precisely because its function is to humanise the consequences of its own exercise, its own existence? If one is reared to a battering, drumming, recurring slogan of *No Surrender*, does it not follow that one single day, even one single enlightened moment of surrender enriches poetry, politics and people? And should not poetry continue to echo that hopeful possibility? In the face of mockery and futility? Even from that same futility and mockery, one learns something. There's no end to learning. Especially from mistakes. Daily bread.

Echoes are a kind of education. They can even educate previous educations. I was a bus conductor in London in 1957, on the 657 trolley-bus from Shepherd's Bush to Hounslow, the Bell. My bus driver had been a Black-and-Tan in Ireland many years previously. He was a pleasant man; he talked to me of his fighting days in Ireland, especially Cork; he knew how hated he and his fellow Black-and-Tans were in my country, but he concealed nothing, or I believed he concealed nothing. I learned something from him: how to listen to someone I was reared to fear and hate, not without reason, for Black-and-Tans had burned my own village, or some houses in it; I knew the families involved. Yet, as I listened to Will Flint, I could hear the decency in the man, I experienced generosity from him, I enjoyed his mature humour; he taught me not to cut him out, not to obliterate him before I heard his voice. He listened to my voice. We worked together, at all hours. We got on OK together. And he was a darned good bus driver.

I think that Will Flint, echoing, helped me write *Cromwell*. What he taught me has still to be learned by a lot of us in Ireland. And, I observe, by myself, at times. Too often for any degree of comfort. Yes, indeed, in spite of the educating echoes. Education is as much a matter of crafty concealment and manipulation as it is of stylish accent and sophisticated expression. Amazing the way ignorance, hatred and prejudice endure and thrive under the educated skin. So much of civilised living is an educated skin. We should be careful how and where we scratch.

My attempts to be faithful to echoes have more or less dictated the structure of this book. At the same time, I've tried not to be rigid in arranging the poems but have tried to let them flow into each other like the talk of friends or efforts to describe recurring dreams. Even, however, as one re-arranges echopoems, these same poems are re-arranging what goes on in one's own head. A poem may reshape a life. Fair enough. Once written, poems have their own lives. They have the right to lead themselves as they see fit. I hope they enjoy every moment. I enjoy their company. I can only hope that they, for the most part, or even the least part, enjoy mine and yours.

It is sometimes said that certain poems have a timeless quality. In my experience of poetry, there are two "times": chronology and intensity; the reality of both of these is measured by memory. Remembering chronology is like relearning the old basic lessons in logic, becoming steeped again in premises, arguments, conclusions, except that now they're called minutes, hours, days, weeks, months, years, decades, centuries, and they're measured by calendars, clocks, watches, computers. Experiencing this chronology of poetry is like experiencing the reassurance generated by solid architecture, strong walls, healthy roofs, dignified windows etc. It gives one a sense of control over time. It is related to technique and form, to rhythms and stanzas, to ideas of discipline and order. This "time" has to do with the logic of passion, the provable sequence of what is happening to us, the discernible and utterable plot in what seems plotless. At its best, it is a formal fire; it convinces the reader's mind and heart. It has the communicable sanity of recognisable shape.

The other "time" in poetry is an attempt to capture the very form of fire itself, it is remembering and therefore repeating moments of intensity, we call it memory but it is rooted in now, like all memory that is passionate and not nostalgic. Memory is not the past, memory is the present working itself out, clarifying itself through its relationship with the past, it is *now*'s version of *then* expressed with honesty, longing and commitment. The haunting power of memory can strengthen as time weakens. In using this concept of "time" to try to structure a book of poems, one is placing one's faith in the ability of the mind and heart *now* to shape the experience of the heart and mind *then*. It is a bridge-relationship across the river of chronological time; and its purpose is to define and place side by side, in the pages of echoes, poems that recognise each other instantly though they've been separated for years like friends or brothers or sisters who went into exile and came back years later, momentary strangers in a once familiar scene, to startle those who stayed behind at home with sharp words or laughing eyes or unmistakable gestures inseparable from their true identity.

11

Then embraces now; now is lit up by then and offers it, in turn, a special light.

In putting this book together, I've opted, on the whole, for time as intensity rather than time as chronology. So, for example, a drowned young woman pulled out of a Dublin canal is neighbour to a translation of an old Irish poem 'The Hag of Beare', a passionately remembering old woman who asserts

> And still the sea
> rears and plunges into me
> shoving, rolling through my head
> images of the drifting dead.

The drifting dead. The sea. A young woman drifting in a canal. Water.

Then follows 'Her spirit', with 'She'd gone to look for water and had found it / in a generous brown fountain'. In the next poem 'Warning', 'Rain of cancer / corrodes the wheat' and

> A strontium snow
> falls
> on Washington, Madrid,
> London, Moscow.

There are connections in poetry quite independent of time, or rather of chronological time. I see these independent connections as little surprising electricities that shock the mind whenever we allow the mind the space to be shocked by small, stabbing connections. I think it was Shelley who said that all poets are trying to write one poem which they never quite succeed in writing. So the entire enterprise is a lifelong enterprise in dedicated failure. But there is the compensation of intellectual, emotional and spiritual electricities that can come only from the poem's own life reaching out to the life of another poem reaching out to the life of another poem reaching out...

I've given one example of poems echoing each other; this book is put together with that belief in poems' echoing lives in mind. Does it work? I don't know. What are echoes, anyway? Whatever else they are, they may well be proof that poems, as the French poet Paul Valéry once said, are never finished; they are merely abandoned. We take them as far as we can before setting them free.

Never finished. Merely abandoned. So what to do? Begin. Begin again.

There's some force in Irish life and culture which tells me that the most vital and sane approach to reality is to begin again. After the troubles, the deaths, the sicknesses, after the rumours, the scandals, the hatreds, the begrudgeries (a popular disease intent on killing off all intelligent fulfilment of potential), after the darkness of disappointment and depression, there comes the realisation that perhaps all these sadnesses are merely the raw material for a new fresh moment of brightness which may in turn lead back to darkness, but not just yet. In that poised moment, poetry lives or wishes to live.

A poem, in my belief, should show darkness as a possible womb of light, and light as a possible signpost on the road to darkness. I see poetry as a passionate balance between these conditions and forces that seem to beget each other, almost to need each other, to combat each other into being, a being that is a primitive rhythm of victory and defeat. This combative rhythm is worked out in individual poems in individual ways. What is beautifully, restlessly and irrationally vivid in this rhythm is the strange, persistent sense of choice which exists like music in it despite the knowledge that darkness and light are locked in each other. Choose, the rhythm says. Choose, in spite of knowledge. When I dare to choose, I choose to begin. To the sight of light at the window, among other things.

BRENDAN KENNELLY

ACKNOWLEDGEMENTS

As well as including new, previously unpublished poems, this book brings together some poems from earlier collections which were not included in my previous Bloodaxe selections, *A Time for Voices: Selected Poems 1960-1990* (1990) and *Breathing Spaces: Early Poems* (1992). Those poems, or earlier versions of them, were originally published in: *The Rain, the Moon* (Dolmen Press, 1961), *The Dark About Our Loves* (John Augustine & Co, 1962), *Green Townlands* (Leeds University Bibliography Press, 1963), *My Dark Fathers* (New Square Publications, 1964), *Collection One: Getting Up Early* (Allen Figgis, 1966), *Good Souls to Survive* (Allen Figgis, 1967), *Dream of a Black Fox* (Allen Figgis, 1968), *Bread* (Tara Telephone Publications, 1971), *Shelley in Dublin* (Anna Livia Books, 1974), *A Kind of Trust* (Gallery Books, 1975), *The Boats Are Home* (Gallery Books, 1980) and *The House That Jack Didn't Build* (Beaver Row Press, 1982).

THE SAME RIVER

The Adventure of Learning

Nakamaro bit his hand and wrote in blood
   of the moon rising
above Mount Mikasa at far-off Kasuga:
   the loneliness of learning.

The talkative Liffey goes stubborn and free;
   rambling, twisting, turning
on its journey to the sea:
   a way of learning.

Across the world a light shines
   binding our lands
together, webs of light linking
   island to island.

Distance. Loneliness. Islands. Seas. Light.
   We go home to each other
through puzzling, winding roads becoming
   mother, father, sister, brother, lover.

We phone, write letters, prowl through books,
   dream of losing, winning
love and fortune. And always, always,
   the adventure is beginning.

Ice

The next day, the papers said
a man stepped out to push his car
and was frozen dead.

I saw the thrush and blackbird,
proud as you like, step kingly to my door,
cocking their heads for bread.

Crusts I threw to the cold singers
who ventured near, like poets
shy to tell their hunger

but quick to take the proffered fare.
Later, by a lake,
I saw a child at the edge where

the ice was just beginning to break;
he wanted to clutch and smash the ice
but someone snapped 'For Christ's sake

draw back, the ice is thin!'
It was, though farther out
seagulls stood on the water's skin

like unperturbed ambassadors who know
just how deep appearances are
and how far they can go

till the ice breaks under their feet.
And I thought
of its purity and threat –

how it kills and cleans, petrifies
and purges, locks, tightens, chokes
and then melts in the sun's rays,

to draw the singers from my door
back to the sky and field;
to let the daring child once more

resume his human privilege
of breaking the rule that says he must
not go too near the edge.

Picturing questions

Who smashed the face of the Egyptian God?
Who opened the child's grave and took the gold chain?
Who stole Beethoven's watch?
    A battered head goes for a walk in the rain.

Sounds

Mice scuttled up and down Mozart's back,
he heard sounds in his head.
He did what the sounds asked him to do,
the seas surrendered their toe-tapping dead.

Baile Bocht

Outside the pub the killer stands
death dumbfounding his victim's eyes.
Dionysiac applause
bombs the Hogan and the Cusack Stands.

A Source

Mad goats leap through his head.
When ice gives way to rain
he drinks the mad goats' milk:
a peaceful man.

A DUBLIN SAUNTER

Citizens of the Night

The toothless old girl sang *A Dublin Saunter*,
ignored the sad look of being ignored
in her daughter's eyes.
The old man chirped 'I think I'll join in,'
and began to sing
as though the joy of the citizens of the night
depended on his quavering fling.
The new boy worked at his first job,
conscience beaming from his forehead
like a miner's lamp in a pretty black pit.
He would be good, really good,
he was ready to sweat blood
in the crowd, getting the hang of it.
Helen Jones from Tullamore
pushed back her chair from the table,
walked to the door. Half-turning her head,
'Not a bad night for love,' she said.

Doorway

Torn cardboard, dumped blanket, crushed cigarette:
James Francie MacDonagh slept here last night
in the cold and the wind and the wet.
Forget.

Children's Hospital

Huge-headed, this petrified freak of clay
stares at the staring visitors bearing flowers,
fragrant tokens of a mute desire to see
the prone ones on the highway to recovery.
Recovery? This one, girl, five years stretched,
looks and looks and says
nothing. Behind her eyes,
bright mornings of her body's freedom.

Intruding rays of sunlight bring
the sky's immaculate benediction
on suffering
that happens in the dullest way
while innumerable children blunder towards
the dangerous light of day.

While things endure or break, while winter comes again
and prowls morosely through dark places,
I read the clammy script of pain
on children's faces.
In Ward 11, Unit 4, St Mary's Hospital,
neatly arranged, paralysed creation
lies limp between the lime-white sheets.

Intruding sunlight hovers on
the unfathomable fruit of God's imagination.

Who Killed the Man?

Was he sitting in a car in a suburban street
reading a paper
or did they shoot him dead
asleep in bed?

No, he is trying to cross a ditch
at the side of a country road.
The truck's headlights select him in the darkness
he's dead clambering
a boy clawing a cliff's face for birds' eggs.

'Fling 'im in the back o' the truck, lads.
We'll ditch 'im near 'is 'ome
mustn't let 'im get lost
make it easy for 'em to find 'im
he'll be 'ome, never more to roam.'

Sixty years from now and then
villagers are gathered to commemorate
the deadinaditch.
Each man has a three-pronged pike.
Each pike bears a flaming sod.
There's a smell of paraffin in the air.
It is the freezing sixth of November,
time to march
the black country road
to the spot
where he was shot.

Yes, he was shot, we all know that,
but who killed the man?
March march march
through the dark dark dark
let the speeches be made
(there's a Big Man here tonight)
the prayers be said for the dead
in freezing November.

What is it they think?
What is it they remember?
What is it they think they remember?
The truck, it is agreed, where he was thrown to bleed
was a Crossley Tender.
Or did they fling him in an ass's cart?
A black ass dragged a dead man's heart.
'Sit up, old boy, don't be so bloody dumb,
ride on an ass's back
into Jerusalem.'

No one stands in the cold too long.
Time for a drink and a song.
Killigan names the dead
lifts his beads on high
appropriate rage and grief in his eye
rattles it out
lust in his throat
Mother of Christ
Star of the sea
pray for the wanderer
pray for me.

It is three o'clock in the morning.
Where are the faces the flames
the passionate words in the freezing dark
the paraffin-smell
the pikes the prayers the naming of names
the wishing of souls to heaven and hell
eternity twisted and tickled by time
that crawled slithered slouched shambled ran?

Who killed the man?

Who killed the man?

Hear the voice of the bomb

Though I nestled in Adam's brain
he'd no time to think of me when
day and night he longed for Eve
and the inane birth of human love.
I wandered through the mind of Cain
and through the hearts of murderous men.
I was the alert, indifferent star
contemplating fields of war.
I was vigilant and relaxed,
the death-arc of a flashing axe,
the candid claymore, the sly sword
killed as they listened to my word:
In the beginning was the Bomb.
In the end will be the same.
The holy images I defiled
became for me a deformed child
unknown, unseen, grotesque, absurd.
In the beginning was his Word:
darkness cannot know the light,
why should darkness want to, since it
palls and shrouds each little mind?
I am what light can't comprehend.
I am the quarrel in the marriage bed
when he longs to choke her dead
and when their children face each other
in hate, I am each murdering brother.
Hatred I love, and still I hate
peacemongers out to pray and prate.
For centuries I strove to be
born but my children ignored me.
Children of hatred love to play
and pitch the world into disarray,
to hear the maimed and wounded scream.
I could have realised their dream
but still they couldn't make me exist
until one morning, hate be praised,
a gifted son made me come true
and down to earth to trouble you,

I'd waited centuries to become
the one and only ultimate bomb,
to turn the seas into seas of blood
to prove the stupidity of the good
to annihilate in one small hour
superb creations of man's power
to show that only fools create
while I'm content to devastate
this earth some potty god has given,
a lunatic substitute for his heaven.
I burn everything for I know well
men work hard to make their hell
to sweat their way from cradle to grave,
graceless, ageless, insatiate slaves.
So I offer myself, my explosive style,
to comfort and beguile you while
you prattle, argue, haggle, chide.
I'm waiting here, your invented god
hoping you find courage at last
to lay yourself and your world waste.
I rest assured you'll do your best.
Who knows? Another world may begin
mythologising grace and sin
and I'll go into the dark once more
till a chosen child will find me there
and his heart will hurt with joy
hearing my heart, Destroy! Destroy!
I rest my case until you find
me ready in your ticking mind.
When I go off, your world goes blind.
Bloodspattered stars can't hear a sound.

Street Verdict

Where the fascist traffic flies
        a man he's never seen before
                judges him guilty with his eyes
                    guilty guilty
judges him guilty with his eyes.

Traffic Lights, Merrion Road, Dublin 4

I

Green orange red
orange green

cars crush by, ruthless
as men wanting to be rich,
Mercedes, Austin, Triumph.

Behind the wheels
faces stern with success
or sour with the possibility of failure.

They stare ahead
seeing nothing on either side,
stiff with the insane concentration of men
going nowhere.

II

Seasons will alter every country
effect a revolution in the buried root
enrich the juice in the thin stem
calm the hysterical sea
with new gold honour the trampled sand.

       Here will be no change
but this quick change of lights.

This change brings silence.

I stand in the middle of silence
like a lost man in a desert
and hear the slaves of history
whining under the whip.

The cars are coffins
trap coffins
bottoms held by hinges at one side
hook and eye at the other.

Disposing thus of dead men
these coffins can be used again.

In this silence the poor do not have coffins
but are buried in their rags.
In some cases
the rags are taken from the corpse
to cover a living body.

Yesterday I saw
five dead bodies
carried through the village in a cart
under a yellow shroud of straw.

A young man reels across my path
laughter boiling in his throat
like a deathrattle,
the fool of hunger.

Captain Harstan
who brought the Eclaire from Africa
told me that on Sunday
he had seen a woman
with a basket on her back
to which was tied
the crooked corpse of her child.

And Dr Trail reported
a father tottering on a road
a rope over his shoulder.
At the other end of the rope
streeling along the ground
were two dead children
he was dragging to a pit.

Mr O'Callaghan of Kilmanus
tells me that corpses
fit well in meal-bags.
Graves are good in ditches
corners of the fields
gardens behind cabins.

Yesterday on the road to Cappagh
I saw a dog
eating the head, neck and ribs
of a man.

Later again
I found part of a human head
gnawed, pocked with blood.
I placed it underground.
In one house
I lifted up a little girl.
Her legs swung and rocked
like the legs of a doll.
Her flesh swam with lice.
Out from the marrow of her bones
scuttled the smell of lice.

It is bad in this place.
No one understands the curse.
Yet word has come that in the mountains
it is worse.

III

I hear the cries of women straggling over stones
or bending in the barren fields,
the cries of men and children too
whose hunger is unknown.
Books will be written
but the hunger is unknown.
Poems will be written, and songs
but the hunger is unknown.

Drunken men will think they tell the truth
statesmen give the bread of explanation
economists suggest solutions
priests wag the finger of warning and accusation
poets celebrate the sacrifice that turns the heart to stone
historians offer facts
wise men nod their theories

but the hunger is unknown.

My brothers will go about the world
in search of money
taking with them
fear pretending to be charm or laughter

insisting on the lie.
Or they'll stay at home
change the barren fields to green
through sunlight rain and hail;
make it nice
and new
and offer it for sale.

Bland reassurances
will calm the blood,
comfort
squat in the bone,
the nightmare melt in the light

But the hunger is unknown.

IV

The light has changed again.
The cars surge forward
like animals unleashed.
Nothing will stop them now.
They'll take the city in their stride.
They drive as though they want to eat it.

It is themselves they eat
to kill the hunger
they do not know they feel
well-dressed, hunched and savage
at the wheel.

A Special Odour

Up from the Sunday morning river drifts
a special odour of corruption,
the Dublin fog of foulness never lifts,
the dead are abed,
the living seek their temples of delusion.

Devil a god would smile to see
the rot beneath the elegance,
the serpent slander that last night stung humanity
lies coiled in sleep.
And now the hour of holy impotence.

If one must offer any prayer
to much-beleaguered heaven –
preserve your sense of humour, be merciful and fair,
for only God's wild laughter
could hope that things will turn out even.

Very soon, I'll up and take a walk
along a route I have not planned,
I'll think of Dublin's treacherous talk
and its malignant silences.
I will not understand.

Not that I give a tinker's curse.
I'll idle by the river's edge and see
the depths where nameless things rehearse
in dark dumb-show, sad human roles –
slimed, active, predatory,

conducting unrecorded slaughter
with viciously accomplished skill
in worlds arrested underwater,
teaching one another
convenient ways to kill.

Portrait

She walks through the grass
(how it glitters in November sun)
searching for something.
Suddenly she drops on her haunches,
picks tiny flowers.
I can see nothing from here
but a girl in a white coat,
a yellow ribbon in her black hair.

She casts a long shadow in the grass.
It tucks itself under her
when she bends to pick the flowers.
It lengthens when she straightens
and follows her
as though to give encouragement.

She is leaving now,
walking off across the fields,
the flowers safe in a small cellophane bag.

Behind her the grass is still
though four yellowy leaves
frisk like children that have no care.

Ghost sculptures of her breath
drift backwards towards the leaves

then vanish in the air.

When he knows he knows

He's had too much to do with drowning
in cold despairing lakes among the streets
where the dead shuffle, afraid of the living,
and the blue beggarchildren cringe in the wet
shade of the bridge protecting the river
from the people. Maybe the river was free
once upon a dream

                      but the people here
thickened the river with poison. I have seen
him warding off the river's invitation
to sleep in its arms, no colder
than the eyes he dares to look at now and then
when he knows he knows too much of drowning:
Sarah Gaire, Billy Rowan, Dipso Craig, Roland
Shaw, Paula Noone. Other women. Other men.

Kind eyes

Over Dublin the full moon
strikes the heavens dumb
enlightening the kind eyes
of the man who split the atom.

The House I Built

(i.m. Jonathan Swift, Founder of St Patrick's Hospital, Dublin)

Last night, in sleep, I built a house. My dreams are true.

This morning, sitting in my bed, I had a fit of giddiness.
The room turned round and round a minute or two.
The fit passed, leaving me sick, yet not plunged in sickness.
I saw Dr Cockburn today, he promised he would do
his best for me, send me the pills did me such good last year.
He also promised me a healing oil for my ear.

For months now, I'm in a bad, dispirited way with deafness,
giddiness, fluxes. Will I ever be able to leave this house?
And what can I do for people who suffer like this
or worse?

'The Bedlam of Paris might be a good plan for that you intend
to found.'
        'It is truly worthy of your great soul.'
'Your heart to bestow is joined in you with a head to contrive.'

I saw what was needed, I worked for that to the end.
The end?
        Cancers? Leprosy? Falling sickness? King's evil?

Sickness struggles to own the world. I want you to live.
Live, do you hear me? Half-living is a safe hell.
The house I built is for souls who would be well.

The Fool's Rod

The city, built in mire and mud,
is refuge for the poor and mad;
the busy man and watchful God
suffer the lash of the fool's rod.

And in the streets, the madmen ply
their holy trade of asking love
with alien eyes, while high above,
shrill seagulls, snowy scavengers
of air, lope, swerve, bank, plunge, make light
of all beneath their marvellous flight –
sewers that rattle, sink and slide
into the fat outrunning tide;
madmen shuffling past blithe lovers
who smile and perfectly rejoice;
past glittering windows, showy flowers,
past silences and small endeavours
and everything without a voice.

Corroding silence is the worst,
has wounded many a noble heart,
made splendid rage and sorrow start
from good Jon Swift, the city's son
and indignation's paragon,
who, loving bitterly, was first
to fight that silence tooth and nail,
to pour the lava of his rage
into the soul of every age,
to break the rod that caused it all.

How strange it is that madmen sing
in sidestreets, rifling litter,
seeking something worse or better
than a passing glance. O may they bring
their queer heart-scalding song
into all armoured hearts, old, young,
indifferent, and may they
give the brutal world that vision
that earns them pity and derision –

lost kingdom gained incredibly,
stretched fields that thrive in sun and wind,
some loveliness whose origin
is built astoundingly within
the deep elysium of the mind.

I name the names of Dublin's mad;
Red Biddy, laughing at the doom
that calls through laneways of the Coombe;
Johnny Gobless, whose heavy tread
is total gluttony for God;
Mad Meg in whose dishevelled hair
the Holy Spirit set a star,
and who, 'tis said, at one time had
such surpassing beauty, all men
who witnessed it were there and then
changed inwardly; Nostromo, tall
and bearded, maddest of them all;
the only mad you'd ever find
who'd spit at rain or clout the wind;
old Zozimus, whose gamey life
became an act of faith in strife;
the Fop, a gentleman from hell,
a defiant rose in his lapel;
Mad Peggie, lifting up her skirts
to remind the world where life spurts
from; then, grabbing one of sixteen
children, cavorts along the street
till at Whitefriars she stands to greet
the Virgin, heaven's fertile queen;
Bang-Bang, who aims the loaded gun
of his defiance at everyone;
and all the nameless ones who talk
to beckoning angels as they walk
the streets with frantic mouths that could
express the marvellous folly of God.

Gibbering tattered souls pass by
raising their strange and distant cry
for something lost in air or ground
that may be sought but never found,
as they, poor souls who crave and moan,
are always seen but never known.

The city, built in mire and mud,
is refuge for the poor and mad;
the busy man and watchful God
suffer the lash of the fool's rod.

The North County Dublinman's Invitation
(from the Irish)

Come on, yourself and myself will hit out for Fingal.
We'll attack every scrap of meat we find there
and steal whatever beef we can lay hands on.
I'll be hanged
and you'll be hanged.
What'll our children do?
Steal meat when the hunger attacks them
like their fathers before them
and try to find a place to lie
where the law won't strut and pry.

Schoolboy

In the city of cynical rain
a schoolboy mouths into the train at Ballsbridge
shouting
'Auschwitz! All change!'

Getting Up Early

Getting up early promises well;
    a milkhorse on the road
induces thoughts of a sleeping world
    and a waking God.

This hour has something sacred;
    bells will be ringing soon,
but now I am content to watch
    the day begin to bloom.

I would only waste my breath
    on poor superfluous words;
how perfectly they wing for me –
    the new invisible birds

who celebrate the light that spreads
    like love to window sills
as morning steps like a laughing girl
    down from the Dublin hills.

Between

Cries at night, laughter in the morning,
gammy sleep between.
Why is one moment sacred? The next obscene?

Johnny Gobless

Gaunt, ungracious in the rain,
fingering a silver chain,
he goes stalking up and down
blessing the unwieldy town.

Madness glitters in his eyes,
weight of sacred sympathies,
and from his lips explode, like birds,
flocks of rapid frightened words.

I think of lonely William Blake
who did a world make, re-make,
who hounded truth until it cried
and laid its head against his side,

whose discontent was made and given
by the amazing hand of heaven,
whose deep divine unhappiness
could only bless, could only bless,

as now this gaunt disordered man
in holy madnesss, knows he can
bless the city in the rain
fingering a silver chain.

Who but poet or madman could
affirm that all there is, is good?
Or with the truth of passion tell
that heaven holds out its hands to hell?

Courage

(i.m. Larry Kelly)

And yes, old dying friend, it's best
to cultivate
a ludicrous largesse of spirit,

show a cocky smile in the face
of dissolution.
I never knew the source of courage

until now.
You know me when I say
it grows from your decay,

flesh flagging towards the box.
Your laughter,
absurd and admirable,

flowers from cankered roots
and is a deeper thing
than I have ever heard from mouths

that do not taste the worm
budging through the blood.
Why is the judgement of rotting lips

impossible to dismiss?
Is this
the only true authority?

Calculators, crawlers, pigs and slaves
abound, you say,
and they will always have their way

until their way fouls to its end,
abrupt or gradual.
Therefore you smile, my dying friend,

and though the terror touches your heart
and every day the ice advances,
the deeper chill

lies in your quiet words.
Last night you stood
at the bottom of the steps

resting for the climb.
I had nothing to say.
You were taking your time

when I saw that courage was something
chuckling and grey,
easy to miss, impossible to follow.

Then you gathered your coat about your throat,
coughed
and went away.

Agreement

'I agree he's not two-faced,' Mahaffy said,
'but what's the good of that
when the one face Nature gave him
would shame a Liffey Rat?'

The Chair

Mickey wanted the chair.
Dickey wanted the chair.
Prickey Hickey wanted the chair.

Mickey had a wife who gave dinners for him.
Dickey had a wife who gave dinners for him.
Prickey Hickey was a bachelor
who screwed the odd bitchelor.

Mickey had written a thesis
on the role of the bullfrog
in the poetry of West-Cork.
West-Cork was a promising Irish poet
with a thing about bullfrogs.
He brooded on bullfrogs till they became
the symbolic essence of his vision.
Much was expected of West-Cork
'capable of a sublime song'
but he took to the bottle
and died young.
Mickey's thesis had gone to the heart of the matter
and now, to round off his work,
he planned a biography of the poet,
a monument of total revelation.
Thanks to a cousinly butcher from Kanturk
Mickey had access to all the unpublished material
and had already completed,
with what seemed to himself
a fair degree of success,
a very rough draft
(though none the less moving for that)
of the tragedy
of young West-Cork.

Dickey was more subtle.
His subject was
pornography in Jane Austen.
With staggering skill, he built his case
on two pieces of evidence,

two sentences out of the novels;
first, 'He ejaculated into her ear',
and then, 'The duke's balls were held in winter'.
The external examiner said Dickey's argument,
conducted with impeccable logic
and with many inspiring insights tossed in,
covered every aspect of pornography
in Jane Austen.
Nothing was left
untouched,
least of all, the external examiner's heart
which practically bled at the contemplation
of this beautifully-structured example
of high academic art.

Prickey Hickey was an interesting case.
He was an expert on sub-plots
in minor Romantic drama
which, perhaps, is why
he went to bed with Mickey's wife
and Dickey's wife,
explaining, when these happy frolics were done,
that two beds are better than one.
A scholar-bachelor must have his fun.
Prickey's mind was a cocked gun,
in the house of learning, a loyal son.
Out of the blue
Mickey and Dickey
withdrew,
leaving Prickey Hickey
the sole candidate for
the chair.

Quitting the world of scholarship
Mickey and Dickey
opened a fish-and-chip shop in Stillorgan
where it is still customary
to eat fish on a Friday,
charming relic of the old faith
which made this life
a disciplined step towards death.

Forgetting West-Cork and Jane Austen
Mickey and Dickey prospered
and were good to their wives
who were good to them
for the rest of their sizzling lives

while
on a summer day
in the pure air
of a very distinguished centre of learning,
surrounded by eminent doctors
row after row, like retired apostles,
Professor Prickey Hickey,
transfigured, debonair,
ascended the chair,
announcing
in language just short of divine
that his interest in the sub-plot would continue,
a lifelong challenge
to his every intellectual muscle and sinew.
Indeed, if the truth were told, such interest
was only beginning.
Clearly, this particular area
was virgin territory.
Like some rich field
awaiting the missioner's zeal,
it was all there
for the winning.

Before

When all the isms have passed away
                you'll see a man astray
on the old stones,
                the old perplexity
                        animating his bones

become rivers bearing the Tall Ships,
a curse or prayer on his half-blue lips,
                no ism now
                to explain it all
                        as he stands
naked, unknowing as he was
                before his climb
                        and fall.

SECRETS IN THE AIR

The Hag of Beare

(from the Irish)

The sea crawls from the shore
leaving there
the despicable weed,
a corpse's hair.
In me,
the desolate withdrawing sea.

The Hag of Beare am I
who once was beautiful.
Now all I know is how to die.
I'll do it well.

Look at my skin
stretched tight on the bone.
Where kings have pressed their lips,
the pain, the pain.

I don't hate the men
who swore the truth was in their lies.
One thing alone I hate –
women's eyes.

The young sun
gives its youth to everyone,
touching everything with gold.
In me, the cold.

The cold. Yet still a seed
burns there.
Women love only money now.
But when
I loved, I loved
young men.

Young men whose horses galloped
on many an open plain
beating lightning from the ground.
I loved such men.

And still the sea
rears and plunges into me,
shoving, rolling through my head
images of the drifting dead.

A soldier cries
pitifully about his plight;
a king fades
into the shivering night.

Does not every season prove
that the acorn hits the ground?
Have I not known enough of love
to know it's lost as soon as found?

I drank my fill of wine with kings,
their eyes fixed on my hair.
Now among the stinking hags
I chew the cud of prayer.

Time was the sea
brought kings as slaves to me.
Now I near the face of God
and the crab crawls through my blood.

I loved the wine
that thrilled me to my fingertips;
now the spinster wind
stitches salt into my lips.

The coward sea
slouches away from me.
Fear brings back the tide
that made me stretch at the side
of him who'd take me briefly for his bride.

The sea grows smaller, smaller now.
Farther, farther it goes
leaving me here where the foam dries
on the deserted land,
dry as my shrunken thighs,
as the tongue that presses my lips,
as the veins that break through my hands.

Tooth missing

you knew her well
nineteen or twenty
tooth missing front of her mouth
looked sad

fond of a drink
really went at it
hit the hard stuff
half-mad with it

hit the heroin
eyes all round her eyes
black as sin

you knew her well
they fished her out of the canal last Sunday
her face kicked in

The song he sang

He plucked a grey hair from his head.
As it floated down the air
he sang the song he sang
the night he was married,
the song that said a dying bird
is never worried.

Her spirit

Once, when both of us were trying to solve the trouble,
I saw her spirit in her face.
It happened at a camping-site
in a dry, humpy country-place.
She'd gone to look for water and had found it
in a generous brown fountain.
Pumping the water into a red plastic bucket
she strolled towards me in the evening light.

That's when I saw the spirit of the woman.

Like the evening, she's easy, deep and bright.
The evening, everything living in the evening
focusses in her strolling figure and shines
through her skin. For a moment, no pain
exists, lost in the focus, the shining.
The water glitters as she sets the bucket down.
She turns her head. The trouble stirs again.

Warning

Her voice
when she spoke –
salmon muscle the waters;
driven from the deep
they drift dead,
bellies whiter than the blank sun overhead

whose light is yet denied
to algae growing on the seafloor
because the waste of countries
pouring, hour by hour,
builds a roof of slime
to strangle the seaflower.

Rain of cancer
corrodes the wheat,
soaks into the grass.
North, east, west and south,
berries steeped in the wind's poison
burst inside the mouth.

Death is pollen
drifting in the atmosphere.
A strontium snow
falls
on Washington, Madrid,
London, Moscow,

on fields where nothing
seems to live,
on villages that sleep inland
or hug wide estuaries
waiting
for what the tides may bring.

Her voice
follows me this morning.
On the tree that reaches to my window
a silent thrush upon a branch
sways
in warning.

Assassin

In its own time and more decisive
than nightfall in December it surges
through you like the sea, love,

love.
When I say everything I mean it
and give

examples. A watch stops at night,
dead skin dissolves in water,
dustmotes dance in sunlight

and settle on the backs of books,
quiet monuments of passionate
men and women who had no truck

with stupid gods but chose the spider's art
becoming rivals of the sun.
Now they play another part

and fructify the dying earth or mingle
with the drowned or lie as much
at one as the chime and the bell

with the heartbeat of their struggle
silent but for voices between covers.
Nothing lives but the riddle

they left like a glove on a chair
or a split horsenut hanging
from its roots in mid-air

feeling the undermining force
of the wind that chills the blood
with ultimate divorce,

cocksure assassin whose aim is perfect,
whose music tilts the axis
when the ocean swells with shipwreck

or hands grow filthy with money
ignoring the infant's fascination
with its own shadow,

a woman feeling in her shrinking wrist
the pulse of terror,
a door closing in November mist.

Conqueror

Huge leaps. Epic soarings of the head.
He glowed within, without. Born to conquer.

'You look fragile,' she said.

Too Near

Do not come too near.
It is the space between
that enables something to grow

and saves us from stifling.
I love to sweep the leaves
from the grass in the garden

and rejoice in the surgeon's skill
when he lops the branch
that keeps the tree from its full

stature.
No, I do not want to hear
everything about you

or possess the secrets
you do not wish to share.
Between us there are secrets in the air

too dear for knowledge,
too true to be fouled by the mind.
This morning I heard sounds of summer

resonant through the door
yet summer keeps itself
to itself

while acknowledging its debt
to winter and spring.
I cherish such reticence,

such private self-definition.
It permits me to see and hear
the best and worst of the current season
and nothing is too near.

Tonight You Cry

Tonight you cry
because you have no friend
and I

am not enough
though I would fill this cold house
with love.

I would lie at your side and bless
every icy spike
of loneliness

in your heart
but it would not suffice
because you suffer a hurt

beyond my reach.
I do not know where friends go.
I can say we lose touch

or forget
or grow beyond
or simply neglect

as I do those flowers whose
names I can never remember
but none of this

explains or consoles your tears
in the room
where shadows gather

about your head
like vague shapes of the lost
stalking through a cloud

in your mind.
Those you have loved
are all buried tonight

at the centre of that cloud.
It is a grey place,
a long stretch of beach in winter

waiting for waves
to run their cold hands
over its face

in a chill ritual of oblivion
advancing
to cover and drown.

Where Women Pray and Judge

After two hundred miles of snow
I walk into the room
where women pray and judge.

We know all about him.

Child of Mary, corpse in blue,
focus of tears and sighs,
love is what I kiss,
and love is ice.

Time for Breaking

When the old man said, watching me
watching the leaves tumble with the river,
' 'Tis like the inside of your head,'

I didn't know for decades what he meant.
In fact, I'd forgotten his words
or consigned them to a corner where they couldn't

be heard until, forty years on, something in me
broke. It was summertime. Not, you'd think,
the time for breaking, but there's no

knowing when the breaking will happen.
Well, the day I have in mind
was sprawled August with other men

who for dreams and reasons of their own
had broken too.
The day started well, the sun shone

on the first shreds of hope for ages,
but towards midday, heaven cracked
in one of its majestic rages

and lashed the well-lashed earth again, again,
while lightning flashed spectacular anger
and thunder forecast in my brain.

I saw the old man watching me
watching the leaves in the river.
Over forty years he stepped slowly

and peered through my eyes.
I don't recall being seen through
so clearly by anyone.

He said ' 'Tis like the inside of your head.'
I hadn't known I'd carried the river in me,
borne it in my blood

these long years. I carry the old man too, closer than ever.
Between us, we make a river, another river,
a laughing angry sunny stormy kind of river.

Angela

So what if they sneer you in the streets
or spit at your father
or slip you the knife in the back
or hiss you to get the boat
now that every wild oat is sown

you needn't give a fiddler's fart
or a withered fig

no one can break you
but yourself alone

Picture

'Why do you like the evening tide?'
'It's like walking into a picture,' she said.

Voice

Pinned. Cold. Shuddering.
'If you wish to reach out,'
voice fades into bird-language,
bat-voice hanging upside down
from the rafter of a house of no time
though once a family warmshone there
not knowing its own light.
'If you wish to reach,'
voice resumes, close, low.
'If you wish,'
pinned. Cold. Shuddering. Voice fades.
'Don't go!' I cry, 'Stay! Don't go!'
Gone.

Irish proverb

Until the duck forgets to swim
and black is the colour of the swan's down
and mad dogs refuse to fight
a woman's mind will flabbergast a man.

Maggie Hannifin's way for women

Tend cheeky flowers of hope
from Stoneybatter to Japan.
Grow your own dope:
plant a man.

Someone Is Hurrying

Someone is hurrying to console another.
As rooms go, hers is warm enough
even in this bitch weather.
Slipping on her blue anorak
running her fingers through her hair
she takes on the traffic
a waiting grief
a crushed love.

You could dub her a willing midwife
scuttling to some aborted mess.
This has been said, and will again.
Out in the streets, she feels unreasonably safe.
A man or a boy with wounded eyes
is waiting. She knows the moment
has come to begin.

Mercy

She walked out then for good.
All he could see was the globe
in the corner of the kitchen.
So much more sea than land,
blue than green.
And there sat squat little comical scandalous Ireland.

All it needed was the sea to go mad one night,
drown the land and everything in it,
every sign and rhyme of women and men.
Where does mercy come from?
He bent, caressed the globe with his right hand,
blue and green coherent again.

Woman in a doorway

Two men went in and out by that door.
The first was a gambler, even his laughter
gambled from one end of the year
to the other, scoffing at before and after,

attentive only to what was happening
now. Now he's gone. The second man
was easy, bit of a loner, took to drinking
till the flesh cartooned itself on his bones.

She never complained. She let them come and go,
live and die in their chosen, enslaved ways,
she lives now as she lived before

they entered and quit her life.
She lays no blame on anyone
but stands, strong and watchful, at her door.

I Didn't Mean to Talk Like This

'Forgive me, I don't wish to talk about it.
I realise I began the conversation.
Something I saw on a TV programme
so well produced, so brutally scripted,
made me wish to talk about this with you.
But now our talk fills me with fear
not for myself only, but for her.
A sheet of paper in a fire, red ash, black ash,
the whole world like that.
People are talking of war again
but can they know what they're saying?
Should we all go mad first?
Would it be better to be mad?
Madness needs no shelter
but goes raw and naked

if nobody takes pity.
Who will pity the black ash of the world?
Who will be left to pity?
She's up in her room playing with books
that years ago taught her to read.
She loves words. Look at that garden
so rough and ready after winter,
it's going to need a lot of work.
I want to plant new grass
and fix wire-netting in the hedge
where that fat white dog sneaks in to dig.
All the cities of the world in ash!
I didn't mean to talk like this
but only final war can follow silence.
Do we really think we can hide in the earth?
Why should it shelter us
who labour to destroy it?
I'm going out to plant fresh grass.
She might like to come too.
That old unruly garden is the place to go.
I'll call up to her now.
She gets such a kick
out of watching things grow.'

A Mad Woman

Her hair blowing about her head
she careers before my eyes,
screaming about her beloved dead
and their deep mysteries.
How passionately she gabs aloud
her mostly incoherent words
at the imperturbable crowd,
at the full air and the wheeling birds,
at the great monuments of stone
and little children at their play,
she shouts, 'Remember you are all alone!
So pray, God damn you! Pray! Pray! Pray!'

Padraig O'Conaire's Daughter
Visits Galway on Her Honeymoon

After the long journey, my husband is asleep.
Tense words of the interview stirring
like restless children in my brain, I lie beside him,
inches from his dream. For better and worse now, I am
part of it. Is that why, a child again, I rise and creep
over to the window, part the curtains, see the city
in the rain? There, in Eyre Square, rain blurring
his head, my father, a statue, sits and broods
as once he did beside the fire, the wet light
of Galway attending his neardistant form.
The rain is getting colder. A vindictive wind cuts
into his back. Wait a moment, father,
I'll come down with a blanket to keep you warm.

Grattan

lifts his right hand
as if to bless
the young woman
drawing a Rembrandt face
on the pavement
under the threat of rain

Speculations

After she passed the headland
why did she turn the car and drive back?
Did she sit for a while looking
at the grey rain caressing grey rock?

When she replied 'Money isn't everything'
what was drifting through her?
Did she turn the pages of the river
to find her peace written in water?

The Destiny of Rats

So you decide to ask the rats to leave the house
and you acquire the Catholic servant-girl
with the nimble fingers and the clear writing
to drop a note to the leader of the rats
asking him to go elsewhere.

                            Wheat, bread
meat, oats, hay, everything has vanished.
Outnumbering rats must be banished
to an accommodating corner of the island. Rats
have always done what certain girls have said.
           A sober man coming down the road
trembles to see half-a-mile of rats, the leader
spelling the way, lucid prose in his mouth.
The man steps into the briary blackberries,
feels the skin of his backside scratched.
The north is purged. The rats are nosing south.

Nora O'Donnell

(for John Healy)

Nora O'Donnell knows how not to die.
This is the steel achievement of blood.
I see her coming out of hospital
pausing a moment at the side of the road
where the first house stood.
                              The first house.
The first garden. The first woman, Nora O'Donnell.
There's work to do, death must be put in its place.
This is acceptable and not without honour.
She is a small town, a fire, Botuney Bridge, a bed
where love is made in the silence it deserves
and you are born to say whatever is in you to say,
angered by the living, enlightened by the dead,
knowing the half-hearted thing is what is killing us.
Let the robin sing its heart out in the bush today.

Hello

Sound of a bell in the wind
Ebe's dancing, she'll dance all night
The future drops in to say hello

The dance is becoming a dance of mirrors
He sees her dance through mirror after mirror
The future's eyes laugh like long ago

Like Maggie Carrig dancing in astonished snow.

Last Kicks

'The power of the world is in the hands
of tired old men,' she said,
'and that's a cosmic sadness. In every land
I've met them, well-dressed, half-dead,
Bored, boring.

Why is this fulfilment a paralysis?
If a corpse could speak he'd be more exciting
than these figures at table, lifting a glass,
or in bed, last kicks of a landed fish
gasping in the dust for its lost element
before it swallows its death and peters out.

Power castrates them long before the finish.
Important, they squat in wealth, blunt
Buddhas of money's ruck and rout.
They trust no one. Themselves they never doubt.

I often laughed in their faces.
They thought they were funny. Dear Jesus!'

In the Rain

I shook at her words
and knew there's no undoing
the tight knot of pain.
She left. I bent to pluck good luck,
a mucky ha'penny in the rain.

Her Laugh

It might have been something Hawley said
as they chatted together at the counter
where the grades weights and the white scales stood
monument to the notion of just measure
for decent people born suspicious
of everything that cannot be proved

but she laughed out of weariness into tears
and continued to laugh after Hawley left.

She was one of those folk who don't laugh much,
whose reasons for silence remain their own
locked property of heart and mind.
Her laugh when it tumbled free was such
a soaring out of work and children
there was nobody she mightn't leave behind.

Miss McKenna

In the house on the hill she lives
                    teaching, learning.
The youngsters' heads are bent to the books,
        the fire is blazing in the grate,
                the two lamps burning.

THE FIELD OF CRIES

A Black-and-Tan

In May, 1957, I met Will Flint
driver of the 657 trolleybus
from Shepherd's Bush to Hounslow, The Bell,
via Chiswick and Brentford
where the gasworks stank
bad as the Liffey
to be redeemed in time
by a sign that said
Come to Kew Gardens
and he told me he'd been
a Black-and-Tan
somewhere in Cork.
'These bloody rebels were everywhere, mate,
'idin' in villages, up in the 'ills,
'idin' in farmers' 'ouses.
Played bloody 'ell with us, they did,
I was lucky to come out alive.
I did some damage meself
but now most of all I remember
the soft women of Buttevant.
Tell you this much, Paddy,
I was never short
of the bit o' crumpet
in the Emerald Isle.
The blokes were out for our skins
but the birds opened up in style.'

Having been reared
to hate the thought
of a Black-and-Tan
the scum of England
more beast than man

I was somewhat surprised to find
how much I liked Will Flint
and his Black-and-Tan talk
warming my heart and mind.

'You've 'eard of the three F's, Paddy,
the three F's for the Irish peasant,
Fair Rent, Free Sale, Fixity of Tenure?
Well, look at the three F's
of the Irish in London today –
Fightin', Fiddlin', Fuckin'!
No wonder you're a race o' bloody wantons!
An' tell me this, mate,
why do you Irish walk our streets
as if you was climbin' fuckin' mountains?
Sometimes I think all you Paddies
shudda stide up in the 'ills!'

Will Flint had thought a little
more than a little.
'I was 'ardly a man
when they sent me to Ireland,
I was a killer
when they brought me back.
Not that it bothers me much.
King an' Country, that's what Flint fought for,
King an' Country, Country an' King.
Well, it must be for somethin'.
I 'ad some good times in Ireland,
drinkin' an' singin' an' lovin',
I'm not complainin',
Then I got 'ome to a small bit o' fuss,
King an' Country looked after me well.
'Ere I am, nearly forty years later,
in the drivin' seat of a bus,
the good ol' 657
goes all the way
from Shepherd's Bush to 'eaven!'

Old Soldier

'I'm eighty-eight,' he said,
    trenchtwinkle in his eyes,
'and though I fought in the worst o' wars
    I'm barkin' lively.

Slogged in the Kimberley Diamond Mines,
    sang on Fiddler's Green
and never, never would accept
    the notion of a has-been.

The years are old, my heart is young,
    there's plenty left to do;
strings of a fiddle, words of a song
    keep me feelin' new.

Complainin' gets ya nowhere.
    Old eyes need a sparklin' sight.
Take me for a walk, young friend,
    to see the Shannon light.'

Ask the Children

'That man fought for the English,' he said.
'Why should he sit there
telling stories to children
gathered about his chair,
stories of his wanderings, his wounds, his stupid war?'

'Ask the children,' she replied
'Why they love him.
Ask the children, if you dare.
Then sit there yourself and try
to tell them a story
born of your ignorant pride.
Your story will tell them who you are.'

Specks

'Call to see him often, if you can.
He's wilder now than ever he was.
I noticed today in Tarbert
When he coughed and spat at half-time
Specks of blood in the grass.'

I Wonder Now What Distance

I wonder now what distance
a man should travel to die;
across a road into a house
or two hundred miles in a car
or take off across the Shannon in the *Marianne*
through the beckoning evening?

Or it might involve a long day's work
with or without a machine:
hands blackened with oil
hair cluttered with dust
he is a search for running water,
he is a worker, he'll be a worker

till the work stops like the brown-faced clock
he bought at an auction for six pounds.
He got it going, it was his pride,
a most harmonious tick all through the house.
Then it gave up, the hands had a crippled look
as though time itself had died.

You made your journey,
it was the right distance for you.
Passing that roundabout, climbing that slow hill,
your body was a house of stifled cries.
The evening opened its mouth and swallowed the traffic.
You closed your eyes.

That's when you saw what you had to see,
your journey being done.
A mountain raised itself from your heart
and shuffled off like a nightmare visitor, hoping
perhaps to impose itself like a shadow of sadness
across the face of the sun

that journeys day into day without complaining,
like yourself at the end, except to say
'I'm very tired, I'd like a long sleep.'
An August morning was an end to weeping.
Peace found you in your sleeping.
Yours, for safe keeping.

Dialogue

The wind is talking to the sea tonight
rough language tumbling from its mouth
enough to give sleeping and waking a right fright.

Up where the nine daughters were drowned –
each one tried to rescue the one before –
you hear the fierce grieving of the wind.

The black rocks brace themselves like youngsters
caught robbing a farmer's orchard.
You never heard such abuse in your life.

Stand there. Pick out the faces in the cliffs.
The wind and the sea hammer them,
the faces take the hammering and the darkness raves.

The sea is talking to the wind tonight,
wild white horses rise and gallop
across black acres of smashing language.

Who has ever heard such dialogue?
They could be lovers or killers
plunging knives in each other's blood.

Because the wise seagulls shelter there,
peace is hiding under their wings
like a frightened boy safe under the stairs.

When he comes out, it'll be morning light.
'Do you know what, Sheefra?' he says to his sister,
'I heard the wind and the sea talking last night.

There's one thing sure: they're not afraid of each other.
Isn't that a godsend – never to be afraid?
All night long. Wild. Real. No fear. Together.'

The Field of Cries

The greyhound tears the hare to pieces
in the field of cries
Nell Hannon says 'tis like a baby
tortured before it dies

> and the priests and the farmers stand around
> listening to the cries
> ascending to the skies
> buried in the ground

the hare is not yet dead
tuggedwrenched from the hound
there's life in the creature still
a man brings on a boy

Let me teach you how to kill
slowly kill

a fair learner, that same boy,
he learns how to kill
slowly kill
he'll be better in the future
so he will
he's a little crude at first
but this will change to skill

> while the priests and the farmers stand around
> listening to the cries
> ascending to the skies
> buried in the ground

and a hound is not a man
and a hound is born to kill
and helps a boy to learn by heart
the words of a man's will

and we watch where something dies
in the field of cries
containing man and boy and hound

    while the priests and the farmers stand around
    still hearing cries
    ascending to the skies
    buried in the ground

The cries repeat themselves

Crackling fun above our heads, seagulls wheel about.

David then: 'A thousand years from now
someone will stand under these black cliffs
and hear the same wild cries.'

The evening tide is going out.

I look at David. Seventy years
pour strength into his words,
laughter through his eyes.

Everything dies yet nothing dies.
Why is everyone no-more? No one, everyone?
The cries repeat themselves. The wild, wild cries.

Roger Boyle

The mass was finished, the priest gone, Roger Boyle
stood in the sanctuary alone
holding by a string the black bag
with his surplice and soutane.

He remembered the smell of wine on the priest's breath,
the talk of God's body and blood.
He wanted to get drunk on the wine.
That October morning, he did.

Stumbling through leaves and chestnuts
down the avenue leading to the main road
Roger Boyle mumbled to the trees
'I'm drunk on the blood of God

and the river is drunk and the bridge is drunk
and so is the sun and the leafy air
and the people stuck into their work
are drunk with Godeverywhere.

And the cold rooms of the school are drunk
and the big grim-eyed man
with the stick in his hand, and my friends' fear
when they stare and listen, trying to understand.'

He came to a roadside fountain,
he watched the water flow,
'O saving water of the world
I know what you know.'

He looked at the grass of Bambury's field
still and morningwet,
'I won't forget this moment, grass of God,
till you forget.'

He turned to the calm river,
the creek, the unchanging mud,
'O mud and river and creek
we live in the blood of God.'

He went to Bambury's hayshed,
he lay in Bambury's hay,
while the calm river flowed past
he slept his God away.

He woke, he sat, he stood, he felt
the hayshed shake
but could not say what his heart felt
now that he was awake.

Company

Naturally they'll look for you outside
in a street or laneway or neighbour's house
behind some bitterly Olympian blockade
but, copping on, you squat in the one place
they're too familiar with to look at.
Under the stairs in the dark is under
their feet climbing to the few rooms where
you might be found, child of the year of the rat,

cornered. Their steps are bloodhounds overhead,
here are old boots, football togs, wellingtons,
rags, bags, company of dust, mud and sand.
And here too the huge bin of paraffin
oil close as your own detonating blood.
A match to that. No more searching. All found.

The Limerick Train

Hurtling between hedges now, I see
green desolation stretch on either hand
while sunlight blesses all magnanimously.

The gods and heroes are gone for good and
men evacuate each Munster valley
and midland plain, gravelly Connaught land

and Leinster town. Who, I wonder, fully
understands the imminent predicament,
sprung from rooted suffering and folly?

Broken castles tower, lost order's monument,
splendour crumbling in sun and rain,
witnesses to all we've squandered and spent,

but no phoenix rises from that ruin
although the wild furze in yellow pride
explodes in bloom above each weed and stone,

promise ablaze on every mountainside
after the centuries' game of pitch-and-toss
separates what must live from what has died.

A church whips past, proclaiming heavy loss
amounting to some forty thousand pounds;
a marble Christ unpaid for on His Cross

accepts the Limerick train's irreverent sound,
relinquishes great power to little men –
a river flowing still, but underground.

Wheels clip the quiet counties. Now and then
I see a field where like an effigy
in rushy earth, there stands a man alone

lifting his hand in salutation. He
disappears almost as soon as he is seen,
drowned in distant anonymity.

We have travelled far, the journey has been
costly, tormented odyssey through night;
and now, noting the unmistakable green,

the pools and trees that spring into the sight,
the sheep that scatter madly, wheel and run,
quickly transformed to terrified leaping white,

I think of what the land has undergone
and find the luminous events of history
intolerable as staring at the sun.

Only twenty miles to go and I'll be
home. Seeing two crows low over the land,
I recognise the land's uncertainty,

the unsensational surrender and
genuflection to the busy stranger
whose power in pocket brings him power in hand.

Realising now how dead is anger
such as sustained us at the very start
with possibility in time of danger,

I know why we have turned away, apart
(I'm moving still but so much time has sped)
from the dark realities of the heart.

From my window now, I try to look ahead
and know, remembering what's been done and said,
that we must always cherish, and reject, the dead.

Missing

Would you doubt him? At the first sign of rain
he's out dragging the ladder from the shed
where in the safe weather it had lain
idle. When the sign becomes a downpour
he stands the ladder against the back wall,
climbs the rain and scours the flooded eaves for
what? Sogged leaves, a starling's corpse, a small
ball green-mossed drop from the sky to the ground

below. Soon as the sun finds heart again
he ransacks every corner of the house
for bits of cardboard, letters, all kinds of paper.
The fire he lights seems part of the man
leaping in and out through his face
so intent, you'd think he didn't miss her.

The Song Inside

The caged bird sang his heart out all day long.
His cage was freedom and his freedom sang.

Inside a shut window hung the cage.
The room resounded with the privilege.

Sometimes I closed my eyes to see
it better, to hear its purity –

note after heart-enrapturing note
pour from the masterful sleek throat.

In silent heaven, a killer spread
his wings – murder in his golden head.

Sovereign in his blue territory,
did, nevertheless, fix his eye

on the caged bird. On high,
poised in murderous mastery,

he watched, watched, knifed the air.
Death whistled, flourished everywhere.

The room darkened like a tomb,
the golden body dispensing doom

found all doom in itself,
hurtling blindly at the glass

that separated this strange pair –
caged singer, golden killer.

Flare of terror. Soon, again, the song inside.
Outside, the hawk was dead.

But it did

(a drama)

A summer's day: an old man sits in the shade,
leathery effigy chewing the cud of dream –
a quiet drama privately staged in his head,
greyed by things that are, saved by things that seem.

A dog lopes into the street where an oily bitch
sweats as she waits, her steaming tongue hanging out.
He circles, smells her, circles again with such
deliberate care, it seems his heart is in doubt.

He mounts of a sudden, expertly spraddles the brute,
his head at her back, scaring the busy flies.
The old man's drama suddenly switches to youth,
the dogs' rhythm increases, he closes his eyes.

In the shade of the castle, the meadowscent was sweet,
the bitch that he mounted then he cannot recall,
the pure daylight, freedom, summery sweat,
rising desire he believed would not end at all.

But it did... and he opens his eyes to the day,
to the dogs that do it, unconscious of living or dead;
a woman passes and turns her eyes away,
he watches, knows there is nothing to say,
the vice of dream tightens his dying head.

A Drowned Girl, the Black Rocks, Ballybunion

Waves' fingers twined a tight noose of death around
her body, destined, until then, to thrive;
when they scrambled her on to the rocks, she looked so young
you'd swear she was still alive.

She didn't look dead, but looked like any girl
at whom you'd throw an admiring glance;
quick brightness in a street, disturbing surprise at evening,
frail truth in the impulse of the dance.

Heroisms happened swiftly; an old man, with bleeding toes,
attempted things impossible alike to old and young;
blew his stale breath between her frigid lips,
too feeble to help stopped heart and water-stifled lung.

Doctor, priest, civilian prayed and probed and tried
to find one reassuring remnant of breath,
as if they couldn't see why a girl in a green swimsuit
should be stretched in death.

There was no flood-tide of grief then, no cold consciousness
of the essential tragedy, yet;
but the curious gaped, mumbled and stumbled
in a way impossible to forget.

Awareness wrapped itself like wet ropes of weed around
        the minds of all,
rocks and beach became a mesmerised room,
and she, turning cold, looked somehow unwanted,
a blue child thrust from an impatient womb.

Various doctors pronounced her dead and everyone stood aside
whilst stretcher-bearers carried her from the rocks to a house
        on dry land;
shortly afterwards, waves' delicate fingers twined white ribbons
        of foam
around her footprints, perfect in the gentle sand.

The Pilgrim

I see a girl climbing the mountain
in a red blouse and blue jeans
rolled up to the middle of her shinbones,
no shoes on her feet meeting the sharp stones,
climbing among rocks, a smile on her face
though her mind may be bleeding from old
and new wounds. In time, she accosts the saint
and in the silence a story is told,
a drop is added to the deepening sea
at the top of the mountain before she
faces down to the world from that brief height.
Below her, for miles around, the fields
are graves for sheep that never saw the Spring light
in grass kneeling to receive the bones and skulls.

The Crossed Country

Small white crosses in the wayside grass
bring the crushed and broken
before the eyes of those who pass

doing a neat sixty, hitting it hard where
commemorative crosses recall others
cutting through the Curragh of Kildare,

who admired the Golden Vale, the midland plains,
flew through the dying towns, observed
the Galtee mountains and the Silvermines,

remarked perhaps how beautiful the land
of quiet houses, rich grass,
but then, suddenly stunned,

ended fatally, noisily,
travellers shockingly still, amid glass,
wood, aluminium strewn horribly.

How honestly they dramatise the dead!
We fly past, placing our faith
as they did, in the god of speed,

glimpsing the green fields that endure,
we who have destinations
risk all that the crosses stand for –

a roadside anonymity,
white symbols to provoke a swift glance
in any traveller's eye,

a certainty surer than highways that bend
through the crossed country to where
all roads end.

Old Year Out

Flung aside like a worn-out boot
the old year falls away;
on every chilly street
nimble fiddlers play
and we begin to forget

four seasons gone, anticipate
the four unborn,
nestling in the future's womb,
children who will turn
our world about, come

with poise, surprise or trouble,
now lie in wait
content perhaps to watch the scene
where fiddlers animate the night
of beating drum and tambourine.

Faces lit with song
dramatise the air;
under the high delighted sky
of scintillating stars, men march together where
another year lies down to die

like some old man who knows it all
and turning his back on everything
the world can do or say,
is glad to hear the voices sing,
the drums resound, the fiddlers play,

while frosty benediction thrills
each fascinating face,
and we accept the strange godsend
that finds life in this dying place,
beginning in this end.

Nineteen Forty-Two

A tangled briar, a bleeding hand,
a berry on a bed of ants,
a boy who sips at fear,
his torn pants.

A Bottle

This is a strong old house, made of stone.
Not the kind you might easily label.
The white-coated chemist, a silent man,
has worked all day in the small
room with the smells of (is it health
or sickness?) filling his head.
He moves intently, almost, it seems, by stealth
till the work is done. In from the red-eyed
winter day where the wind and the rain
vie with each other to humiliate the town
shuffles the farmer, old and strong with caution.
If his body were all pain he'd give no sign.
A few words with the chemist and he's gone,
his pocket bulging with a bottle marked Poison.

The Swan's Curse

My oiled neck, crippled wing
tell of a money king.
My fogged eye, obscene down
prove his crown.

He has a nice family life.
May he fuck a cancered wife
to bear him a cancered child
by whom swans are defiled.

Curse o' Jesus, curse o' Pan
on that man
who would foul me from my place.
May shame pock his face.

Who does not see this
may he never know bliss.
May his kind abuse him.
May the grave refuse him.
May his God vomit him.

LATE IMITATORS

Saint Augustine on God

What do I love when I love God?
   Not a thinker, profound and wise,
not a bright shock of light
   mesmerising my eyes

not a song capturing my heart
   not flowers and spices
not bread and honey
   not limbs loved all night:

I love none of these when I love my God.

   Yet I love a kind of light
a kind of voice   a kind of scent
   a kind of food   a long embrace

when I love God:

light, voice, scent, food,
embrace of this inner man
whose fire defines who I am
and nothing can put down.

A voice speaks defying time
   a fragrance concentrates no wind can break
a flavour lives no hunger kills
   in a strong embrace that cannot grow weak:

it is this I love when I love my God.

   I asked the earth first, 'Are you this?'
The earth replied 'I am not it.'
   All things on land spoke with this voice.

I asked the sea, pit of creeping things
   without a name. They said
'We are not God, go somewhere else,
   ask what is above your head.'

I asked the winds, the winds replied
    'Anaximenes? He was wrong.
We are not God.' I asked moon, stars, sun.
    'We are not God' came sharp and strong.

I asked nothingeverything, 'Who is my God
    summoning me with such a call?'
All voices became one voice. It said
    'Who made us all?'

Saint Augustine's toe

He heard her pray that her soul
would be so pure 'twould make the snow look black.
She leaned forward and kissed
Saint Augustine's toe.

A hard man, by all accounts, quick
to take a rub o' the relic himself
before he repented and said his prayers.

She's off to get a chicken from the butchers.
Nine mouths to feed, nine bodies and souls
to fight another winter.

Taste

Augustine said poetry is the devil's wine.
He drank it often in his youth.
It tasted fine.

Ecstasy

When it comes to ecstasy, she said, language
is a three-legged greyhound flumping after
a deer.

His mind is a dump of black wonder.
Do poets rape paper?

Terms and Conditions Apply

Welcome to *The Kavanagh,* a new Big House, cost a million,
nobody shouted stop.

(Why should they, darling, shut your trap,
study the sacred Property Supp.)

'On many occasions I literally starved in Dublin.
I often borrowed a "shilling for the gas"
when in fact I wanted the coin to buy a chop.'

Columkille the Writer

(from the Irish)

My heart is jacked from writing.
My sharp quill shakes.
My thin pen spills out
blood from my stormy lakes.

A stream of God's own wisdom
flushes my hand.
It blesses the waiting page.
It blesses where holly is found.

My thin pen is a traveller
in a world where books are waiting.
Who dares to see? Say? Who bothers to listen?
My heart is jacked from writing.

Thérèse

She's out on the beach with the children having fun.
Atlantic breakers rear and scatter
foam like blessings in the sun.
Sea-breezes play in her tidal hair,
her eyes enjoy the sea, she looks and listens
to the inexhaustible Atlantic prayer
flung like rose-petals over sand and stones
to reach a man in a dark room where

his gangrenous tongue is healed. And then
her mind is arid-empty, her heart a dark
pit riddled with demons' mocking cries.
        Sick now, she persists, life nearly gone.
Eternity is time to do more work.
All tired, she writes a letter to love. Love replies.

Dying she grows a rose that never dies.

Saint Brigid's Prayer

(from the Irish)

I'd like to give a lake of beer to God.
   I'd love the Heavenly
Host to be tippling there
   for all eternity.

I'd love the men of Heaven to live with me,
   to dance and sing.
If they wanted, I'd put at their disposal
   vats of suffering.

White cups of love I'd give them
   with a heart and a half;
sweet pitchers of mercy I'd offer
   to every man.

I'd make Heaven a cheerful spot
   because the happy heart is true.
I'd make the men contented for their own sake.
   I'd like Jesus to love me too.

I'd like the people of Heaven to gather
   from all the parishes around.
I'd give a special welcome to the women,
   the three Marys of great renown.

I'd sit with the men, the women and God
   there by the lake of beer.
We'd be drinking good health forever
   and every drop would be a prayer.

Sebastian

The arrows harass him like winter pains
frequent and grim
and yet it seems that he ordains
they riddle him

as if they did not split the air
whistling for blood
but that their heads are buried where
Sebastian would.

One angry shaft
explodes inside his groin –
grotesque, excruciating part
of a sure design

in which he twitches, writhes, succumbs
with gasps that seem to bless
the point of all such martyrdoms –
man's nakedness.

His consummating fall
proves his mortality well;
destruction proves him, most of all,
indestructible.

The Tree's Voice

Felled at the forest's edge,
hewn, yanked, chopped, shaped until
I governed this noisy hill,
I am the scene of crime and privilege.

I carried him
who'd caused good sap to flow like blood
through leaf, branch, trunk, eternal bud,
made strong each limb;

watched me grow sturdy, sent
sun and wind and rain enough
to hint at every miracle of love.
I became his punishment.

Wan, as was predicted, the young hero stepped
up to me, stopped at my unwithering root;
I dumbly bore my awful fruit
while all creation wept.

Party

Joseph made the chairs and table
with customary skill and care
Mary welcomed in the neighbours
Jesus lit the fire

Lislaughtin Abbey

Flashing starlings twist and turn
    in the sky above my head,
while in Lislaughtin Abbey lie
    the packed anticipating dead.

Silent generations there
    that long had bent the knee
endow the Shannon with the grace
    of reaching to the sea.

Swollen by the rich juice of the dead
    the Shannon moves with ease
towards a mighty union with
    Atlantic mysteries.

But though the river sweeps beyond
    each congested bone,
its currents do not swirl towards
    a resurrection,

any more than starlings do
    that, fearing death this winter day,
create small thunder in the sky
    and shelter where they may,

ignoring green Lislaughtin where
    subtle shadows pass
through shattered altars, broken walls,
    the blood of martyrs in the grass,

into the ground that winters well
    and blossoms soon or late,
preserving patient multitudes
    who are content to wait

till they at last disturb the stones,
    the fox's lair, the starling's nest,
to cry out with the howling damned,
    to wonder with the Blessed,

to hear the word for which they wait
    under the coarse grass
the meanest blade of which assists
    in what must come to pass,

to see why silent centuries
    have finally sufficed
to purge all in the rising flood
    of the overflowing blood of Christ.

Restless at the gate, I turn away
    groping towards what can't be said
and I know I know but little
    of the birds, the river and the dead.

To imitate the sun

To imitate the sun
is to let the light become
dream-architect, image-maker
working in the dark to shape
maps tracing the spirit's journey
forward to its beginnings
of infinite simplicity.

A Man I Knew

(i.m. Patrick Kavanagh)

1

'I want no easy grave,' he said to me,
'where those who hated me can come and stare,
slip down upon a servile knee,
muttering their phoney public prayer.
In the wilds of Norfolk I'd like to lie,
no commemorative stone, no sheltering trees,
far from the hypocrite's tongue and eye,
safe from the praise of my enemies.'

2

A man I knew who seemed to me
the epitome of chivalry
was constantly misunderstood.
The heart's dialogue with God
was his life's theme and he
explored its depths assiduously
and without rest. Therefore he spat
on every shoddy value that
blinded men to their true destiny –
the evil power of mediocrity,
the safety of the barren pose,
all that distorted natural grace.
Which is to say, almost everything.
Once he asked a girl to sing
a medieval ballad. As her voice rang out,
she was affronted by some interfering lout.

This man I knew spat in his face
and wished him to the floor of hell.
I thought then, and still think it well
that man should wear the spittle of disgrace
for violating certain laws.

Now I recall my friend because
he lived according to his code
and in his way was true to God.
Courage he had and was content to be
himself, whatever came his way.
There is no other chivalry.

Not a word

The greatest poet who ever lived
never wrote a word

but was overheard
to say

Late Yeats

Our greatest poet was worried
    rather late in life,
'I can't have sexual intercourse
    with lover or with wife.'

A friend said 'Go to London
    for a monkey's juicy glands.'
'My sexual future,' mused the poet,
    'lies in Eugene Steinach's hands.

Steinach's operation
    will renew my sexual power,
my poetry will be rammed with life
    as I near my final hour.

A poet's life is poetry
    his blessing and his curse
and should his penis shrink and droop
    so will his verse.

Verse-making and love-making
    inspiringly connect.'
Then love and verse exhorted Yeats,
    'Erect, old man, erect!'

Was Steinach's op. successful?
    Yeats, when he came through,
believed his penis hardened.
    His poetry hardened, too.

The poet became a singing Will,
    ladies grew uncouth
for the youngold man who'd not accept
    the body's stinking truth.

And as rotten death iced nearer
    with all its rotten wrong
the poet loved with his dying breath
    and spilled his living song.

Heart

I cannot thrive outside my cage,
those red bars that make all possible.
Pluck me out from this

I am a dead bird in the dust.
A passer-by might lift the body by one wing
and comment on lost flight,

days of freedom in the air.
He would be wrong because
my freedom is my cage

here in this bloodworld
of unresting rivers
flowing to the sea beyond the skin

beyond the loves and conflicts
and the relish of uncertainty.
I have such a life (limited, it is true)

that you should know
I beat for you.
I beat the storms for you

with rhythm
the world would ask you to relinquish
because the world's a dumb

stump lacking blood but not malice.
Listen to my music,
it is yours also,

why do you turn away?
Look into me, hear me.
I am all you have to say.

Begin

Begin again to the summoning birds
to the sight of light at the window,
begin to the roar of morning traffic
all along Pembroke Road.
Every beginning is a promise
born in light and dying in dark
determination and exaltation of springtime
flowering the way to work.
Begin to the pageant of queuing girls
the arrogant loneliness of swans in the canal
bridges linking the past and future
old friends passing though with us still.
Begin to the loneliness that cannot end
since it perhaps is what makes us begin,
begin to wonder at unknown faces
at crying birds in the sudden rain
at branches stark in the willing sunlight
at seagulls foraging for bread
at couples sharing a sunny secret
alone together while making good.
Though we live in a world that dreams of ending
that always seems about to give in
something that will not acknowledge conclusion
insists that we forever begin.